SPRINGSTEEN
SPRINGSTEEN
SPRING
SPRING

BRUCE SPRINGSTEEN

by
Marty Monroe

An Iron Brigade Production

robus books
P.O. Box 13819
Wauwatosa, WI 53213

Research editor: Jeff Tamarkin
Coordination: 2M Communications Ltd.
Photo Research: Amanda Rubin

ISBN 0-88188-325-5

PHOTO CREDITS

Richard E. Aaron/Thunder Thumbs: 8, 10, 30
Robert A. Bentchick/Star File: 15, 45, 46, 47
Larry Busacca: Back Cover, Inside Back Cover, 12, 14, 20, 36,
37, 39, 40, 42, 43, 58
Fin Costello/Retna Ltd: 22, 29, 49
Ed Geller/Retna Ltd: 44
Bob Gruen/Star File: 62
Laura Levine: 3, 63, 64
Ross Marino: 9, 24, 27, 55, 56
Jeffrey Mayer: 16, 21, 51
Paul Natkin/Photo Reserve: Poster, 19, 23, 41
Anastasia Pantsios/Star File: 5, 6, 7, 32, 33, 34, 38, 48, 53, 59
Ebet Roberts: Front Cover, Inside Front Cover, 17, 25, 50, 52
David Seelig/Star File: 18
James Shive: 1, 11, 13, 26, 28, 31, 35, 54, 57, 60
Bob Sorce/Retna Ltd: 4

WELCOME TO THE SHOW

BRUCE SPRINGSTEEN

Rock 'n' roll has produced kings and queens and many a court jester, but there is and always will be only one Boss. His name is Bruce Springsteen.

From the moment he hits the stage to the last exhilarating, exhausted second over four hours later, his audience is nearly reeling from the mesmerizingly intense passion of his performance. Bruce gives the screaming thousands a show unlike any other in the history of rock. Though many have claimed that he is most likely the living embodiment of the founding spirit of rock 'n' roll, Bruce remains completely without guile, unself-conscious, and true to himself and his muse. He is devoted to his audiences, to the indefinable yet all-powerful spirit in the night that propels him on to another gig, another riff, another smile at the Big Man and his E Streeters, another line of love, another enraptured fan.

Bruce's lyrics display a sensitivity that has made him one of rock 'n' roll's most intelligent and perceptive songwriters. Using many of the themes of the life he has known so well—the struggle to earn a decent living, the joy of cruising with the top down and the radio on, the undermining passions of human nature, the knowledge that we are born to run—Bruce's music has an appeal that transcends all classes. "There's a little barrier that gets broken down, a consciousness barrier," he has said. "Rock 'n' roll reached down into those homes where there was no music or books or anything. And it infiltrated that whole thing. That's what happened in my house." And Bruce is able to elevate the experiences and emotions common to all of us with a maturity and insight rarely found in popular music. "You've always got to remember," Bruce has claimed, "rock 'n' roll's never been about giving up. For me, for a lot of kids, it was a totally positive force . . ." What makes Springsteen so powerful at heart is his ability to convey a universal message while still making you dance till you drop— and love every minute of it.

Just when you thought rock music had lost its fire, Jon Landau, music critic and now manager/producer of Springsteen, summed it up perfectly with the infamously prophetic line: "I saw rock 'n' roll's future and its name is Bruce Springsteen."

Bruce wrote the song "Factory" about the place where his father worked. When he recently returned to it, the building had been shut down.

BRUCE SPRINGSTEEN IS THE BOSS

It's been no overnight success for Bruce Springsteen—he's paid enough dues. He was the victim of hype as the "next Dylan" when his first album was released, suffered the effects of litigation with his original manager that prevented him from recording for over a year, and worked ceaselessly in the studio in his drive for perfection. But he's also been rewarded after those years of struggle with a loyalty from his fans much like the loyalty he has shown the members of his band and the locals of southern Jersey. He's put Asbury Park, N.J. on the map for millions around the globe, even though he was born and raised in Freehold, N.J.

After playing in various bands, Bruce formed the E Street Band in the early seventies and was signed to Columbia Records. His first album, **Greetings From Asbury Park, N.J.**, was released in 1973 to critical acclaim, although it was not a huge chart success. It was followed by **The Wild, The Innocent & The E Street Shuffle** in 1974. But by 1975, the breakthrough success of **Born To Run** established Springsteen as a major rock contender. In an almost unprecedented event in the history of popular culture, he landed simultaneously on the front covers of both **Time** and **Newsweek.** Now Bruce was truly off and running.

The follow-up album, **Darkness On The Edge Of Town** was also a huge success, and Bruce went on to release the 2-album set, **The River,** which spawned his first Top 10 single, "Hungry Heart." His next release, the somber all-acoustic **Nebraska,** may have perplexed some of his fans, but Bruce has more than enthralled them with the 1984 release of **Born In The U.S.A.** This album quickly went platinum and featured the #2 hit, "Dancing In The Dark" as its first single.

Springsteen's reputation as a must-see performer was established early in his career, and by the end of the seventies his concerts were sellouts, tickets were coveted items, and lucky fans were treated to hours of exuberant rock hits coupled with soul-wrenching ballads, led on by the Boss's sheer indefatigable exuberance.

If ever Bruce Springsteen were blinded by the light, it would be that of his own incandescence—his triumph on vinyl and on stage—his magical ability to touch people's hearts.

Bruce on his fans: "They work all week and sometimes stand in line for tickets for ten hours. So we always play our best for whoever is there. You don't lay back in this band, and that is why people come to see us—because something is going to happen. Something—somehow, someway."

ABOUT THE BAND

The 1984 tour lineup (left to right): Clarence Clemons, Max Weinberg, Patti Scialfa, Garry Tallent, Nils Lofgren, Roy Bittan, Danny Federici, and their fearless leader, Bruce Springsteen.

CLARENCE CLEMONS

At 6'4" Clarence has certainly earned his nickname "The Big Man." Only his monster saxophone playing approaches his height in terms of hugeness. Clemons played football in college and even tried out for professional teams before a knee injury forced him to concentrate on his music. Originally from Norfolk, Virginia, Clemons (born in 1942) began his music career by singing in church. He got his first sax as a Christmas present from his father when he was nine years old. After having played with the likes of James Brown, he met Bruce Springsteen on an Asbury Park street when his car broke down—and he's been with the Boss ever since. Recently The Big Man recorded his first solo album, **Rescue,** and put together a band called the Red Bank Rockers to play when the E Street Band isn't touring.

GARRY TALLENT

The bassist of the E Street Band originally played guitar. Garry is a fanatic record collector with a special love for the rockabilly music of the fifties, and he keeps a well-stocked jukebox in his home. He's been a member of the E Street Band since the first album, **Greetings From Asbury Park, N.J.**

STEVE VAN ZANDT

Although he recently left the E Street Band to pursue his own career, guitarist Steve Van Zandt—known to fans both as Miami Steve and Little Steven—was always one of the most popular members of the Springsteen troupe. A longtime friend of Springsteen's, he produced the early records by fellow Asbury Park rocker Southside Johnny, and didn't become an official member of the E Street Band until **Darkness On The Edge Of Town.** His current band is called Little Steven and the Disciples of Soul.

DANNY FEDERICI

The E Street Band's organist has been with Bruce since the days when Bruce fronted a heavy rock band called Steel Mill. Known as "The Phantom," Federici grew up in Passaic, New Jersey, closer to Manhattan than Asbury Park—yet when he met Bruce there was no doubt that he was one of the guys. Although he plays the organ in the band, Danny has also played accordion with Bruce. His playing gives the E Street Band an added measure of soul.

ROY BITTAN

The pianist had the difficult job of replacing jazz-trained David Sancious in the E Street Band. When he made his first appearance on the **Born To Run** album, there was no doubt that Roy Bittan was a masterful player in his own right. In fact, Bruce calls him "The Professor" because of his technical proficiency. Roy grew up in Far Rockaway, New York, making him the only non-Jerseyite in the band (until the 1984 tour) and he once played in the touring company of the show **Jesus Christ Superstar.** His distinctive keyboard work is crucial to the E Street sound.

MAX WEINBERG

The New Jersey boy became hooked on rock 'n' roll when he was a kid and never looked back. He took up the drums and even studied with a master rock drummer, Bernard "Pretty" Purdie, who had played on many of the soul records Max loved. He joined the band for the **Born To Run** album and has helped give not only that record but all subsequent efforts an extra dose of power. In concert, Max is the dynamo who fuels the Boss. "Mighty Max," as he's called, recently wrote a book, **The Big Beat,** in which he interviewed great drummers of rock 'n' roll.

NILS LOFGREN

A major rock guitarist and performer in his own right since the early seventies, Nils Lofgren joined the E Street Band in 1984 when Miami Steve Van Zandt left to tour with his own band. Lofgren met Bruce Springsteen back in the late sixties when they both auditioned for a concert booking at the Fillmore East on the same night. His earliest success was with the band Grin, and he later went on to join Neil Young. He subsequently began a successful solo career, highlighted by the 1976 album, **Cry Tough.** His guitar skills are legendary among aficionados of fine musicianship and he added muscle and new instrumental insight to the E Street Band's live sound when he joined the '84 tour.

PATTI SCIALFA

Fans of the E Street Band received a pleasant surprise during the 1984 tour when Patti Scialfa appeared on-stage to sing with Bruce. Patti, 28, first auditioned for Springsteen when she was 17, long before the E Street Band even existed. Bruce told her to stay in school and come back when she had an education, so she did! In the meantime, she sang with fellow Jersey sensations Southside Johnny and the Asbury Jukes and with local N.J. bands. "Having a woman up there with us gives it more of a feeling of community," Bruce has said.

In 1975 Bruce made the covers of **Time** and **Newsweek** simultaneously. Said his father: "Better you than another picture of the president."

"No two of Bruce's shows are ever alike. Even when
the songs are the same, which they hardly ever are,
Bruce brings something different to every one."
—Rock critic Dave Marsh

Now, this is what you call gettin' down!

CHRONOLOGY

1949 Bruce Springsteen is born on September 23 to Adele and Douglas Springsteen. (His sister Ginny is born a year later, and another sister, Pam, is 13 years younger.) Bruce lives in his birthplace—Freehold, New Jersey—until his late teens.

1956 Like millions of Americans, Bruce watches the amazing Elvis Presley on **The Ed Sullivan Show,** and it's a revelation. Even though his mother buys him a guitar, he doesn't learn to play it for years.

"Whenever a song's got that life, that ability to move you, that's very important."

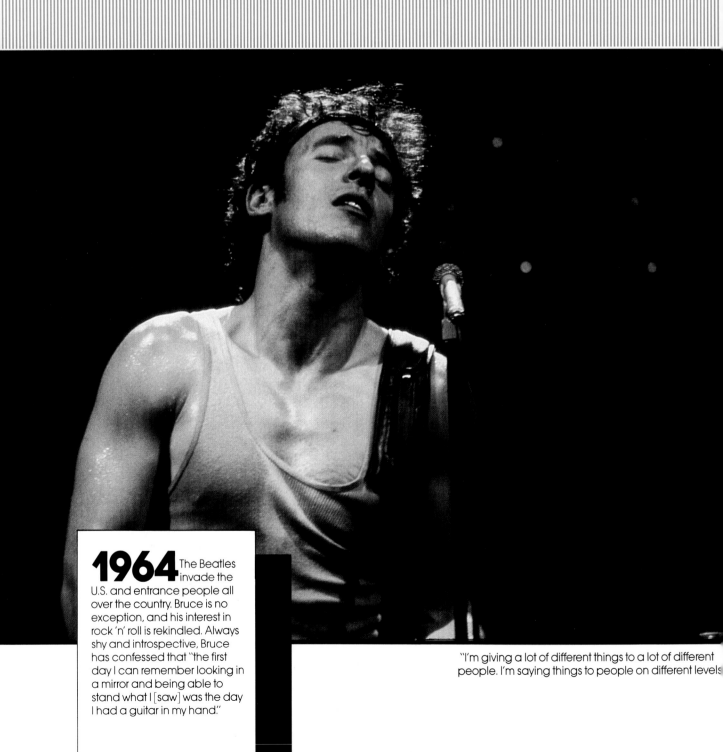

1964 The Beatles invade the U.S. and entrance people all over the country. Bruce is no exception, and his interest in rock 'n' roll is rekindled. Always shy and introspective, Bruce has confessed that "the first day I can remember looking in a mirror and being able to stand what I [saw] was the day I had a guitar in my hand."

"I'm giving a lot of different things to a lot of different people. I'm saying things to people on different levels

1965 Springsteen is now 14, and he learns that a local 5-piece beat group called the Castiles is looking for a guitar player. He cajoles their manager, "Tex" Vinyard, into giving him a chance, and is told by Vinyard to learn some songs and return when he has mastered them. To the surprise of Tex and the Castiles, Bruce returns the next day with note-perfect renditions of 5 songs. "He knocked my ears off," remembered Vinyard, "and he learned them by listening to the radio." Bruce stays with the Castiles through 1967.

Springsteen's latest album, **Born In The U.S.A.** , sold a million copies within two days. Every date on his 1984 tour sold-out in record time.

1966 On May 22, the Castiles make their only recording, a single with two songs, "That's What You Get" and "Baby I," written by Springsteen and the group's main vocalist, George Theiss. The recording is never released.

Vocalist Patti Scialfa added her harmonies on the 1984 tour.

1967 The Castiles audition for the Cafe Wha, a popular night club in New York's Greenwich Village. The proprietor is so impressed that he makes the Castiles the house band. Unfortunately, the group disbands during the summer when the boys graduate high school and move on to other things. Springsteen joins a heavy rock group called Earth, influenced by the likes of the Doors and Cream. Bruce begins playing in the Asbury Park area of New Jersey, and when Earth disbands he begins working with musicians who are part of the Asbury Park "scene," such as Vini "Mad Dog" Lopez, Miami Steve Van Zandt, Danny Federici, and others. He calls his new band Child.

"My songs are all action songs. They're about people at that moment when they've got to do **something,** do **anything.** There's no halfway in my songs, no room to compromise."

1968 Child becomes Steel Mill, a heavy blues-rock band, and earns a reputation as one of Asbury Park's best bands. Springsteen drops out of college to pursue music full-time. The following summer Steel Mill travels to California to try their luck. There they draw rave reviews when they appear at the Jefferson Airplane's Matrix club and they're offered a recording contract from Bill Graham's Fillmore Records, which they turn down.

Bruce was influenced by the great original rock 'n' rollers of the fifties and sixties. Sometimes he even starts to **look** like Elvis Presley!

1971 Having returned to New Jersey, Springsteen dissolves Steel Mill and forms a ten-piece group featuring horns and girl singers. While rehearsing that group, he forms yet another band, Dr. Zoom and the Sonic Boom, which plays only three dates. The ten-piece band, known as the Bruce Springsteen Band, plays only two gigs after six months of rehearsals. However, in that band the seeds are sown for the future—the group includes bassist Garry Tallent, keyboardist David Sancious, guitarist Miami Steve Van Zandt, Lopez, and Federici. During a break at one of their shows, Bruce and Miami Steve meet a saxist named Clarence Clemons. Bruce decides to try as a solo act for a while until he can get another band together.

"Sometimes you can't tell where Clarence ends and his sax begins. He's a pussycat."—Bruce

1972 In May, Springsteen signs a long-term management and song publishing contract with Laurel Canyon Productions. His manager, Mike Appel, arranges a meeting with John Hammond of CBS Records, who had discovered such greats as Bob Dylan and Aretha Franklin. Upon hearing Bruce sing his song "It's Hard To Be A Saint In The City" accompanied by just an acoustic guitar, Hammond is impressed. "I reacted with a force I've felt maybe three times in my life," he said. "I knew at once he would last a generation." In June, Bruce Springsteen signs a 10-album deal with Columbia.

Bruce and Jackson Browne were good friends long before they teamed up to perform at the "No Nukes" concerts.

1973 Bruce Springsteen records his first album for CBS, **Greetings From Asbury Park, N.J.,** with his friends from Asbury Park: Tallent, Federici, Sancious, Clemons, and Lopez. Miami Steve makes only a cameo appearance on the song "Lost In The Flood." Columbia begins hyping Springsteen as a "new Bob Dylan," which almost ruins his budding career. The band officially becomes known as "Bruce Springsteen and the E Street Band."

"I'm not into people screaming at me. Once they do that, it's over. I'll go back to playing the small clubs."

1974 Springsteen's second album, **The Wild, The Innocent & The E Street Shuffle,** is released. Springsteen receives glowing reviews from critics and begins to overcome the hype which almost drowned him. His live concerts gain a reputation as being among the most exciting in all of rock music. Unfortunately, radio play is slow and the album does not sell in great quantities. Rock critic Jon Landau declares after witnessing a show, "I saw rock 'n' roll's future and its name is Bruce Springsteen." CBS seizes on the quote for a massive advertising campaign. Landau and Springsteen become friends and Landau eventually becomes Bruce's producer and manager.

Veteran guitar hero Nils Lofgren took over the spot vacated by Miami Steve for the 1984 tour.

1975 Sancious and Lopez leave the E Street Band and are replaced by pianist Roy Bittan and drummer Max Weinberg. Work begins on a new album early in the year, but sessions drag on slowly. Landau takes full control as co-producer with Bruce, and "Born To Run" is released as the first single. In October, the album **Born To Run** is released. It becomes an instant classic, reaching #3 on the album charts and delighting not only fans and critics, but radio programmers as well. Springsteen establishes himself as one of the great all-time American rockers, with a passion and commitment rarely seen since the early days of the genre. The mushrooming attention paid to Springsteen results in simultaneous cover stories in **Time** and **Newsweek,** leading to further accusations of overhype, but cementing Springsteen's name in the rock community.

Springsteen composed his **Nebraska** album on acoustic guitar and decided to release the raw tapes as an album.

1976 Legal problems between Springsteen and manager Mike Appel prevent Springsteen from recording throughout the year. Appel seeks to bar Springsteen from recording with Landau as producer, while Springsteen seeks to be released from his management contract with Appel. The court matters drag on until May 1977, and the band fills up the non-recording time by extensive touring.

"If you like rock 'n' roll you gotta like our band. We're a real American band." —Bruce Springsteen

1977 On June 1, only five days after the legal matters with Appel are settled (Bruce is released from his contract and Appel gains a cash settlement), Springsteen returns to the studio with Landau. Meanwhile, Manfred Mann's Earth Band has a #1 hit with Springsteen's "Blinded By The Light." Other artists to record Springsteen's songs in this period include Patti Smith, Robert Gordon, and the Pointer Sisters.

"It's a lot of work being in this band, but we're doing something we like. We always considered ourselves to be way in front with the whole ball game."—Bruce

1978 The fourth Springsteen album, **Darkness On The Edge Of Town,** is finally released in May. On May 23, Bruce Springsteen and the E Street Band, now including Miami Steve as a permanent member, embark on a major tour of arenas and theaters. The tour lasts until New Year's Day and takes in 86 cities for a total of 109 shows. The album is another huge hit.

Sometimes even The Boss has to sit down on the job.

1979 Springsteen joins with such artists as Jackson Browne, Crosby, Stills and Nash, and Chaka Khan for the "No Nukes" concerts presented by M.U.S.E. (Musicians United for Safe Energy) at New York's Madison Square Garden on September 22 and 23. Although the crowd is shouting "Bruce," some artists are mistakenly given the impression that they are being booed at! The concerts are later released as a film and album, with Bruce's medley of Mitch Ryder hits of the '60s receiving the most airplay.

"You can tell that the guys in this band don't have a whole lot in common, but somehow the music cuts through all that."—The Boss

1980 The two-record set, **The River,** is released in October and quickly becomes Springsteen's biggest seller yet, topping two million copies and hitting number one. The single "Hungry Heart," puts Bruce in the Top 10 for the first time.

"To me, rock 'n' roll was the only thing that was ever true, the only thing that never let me down."

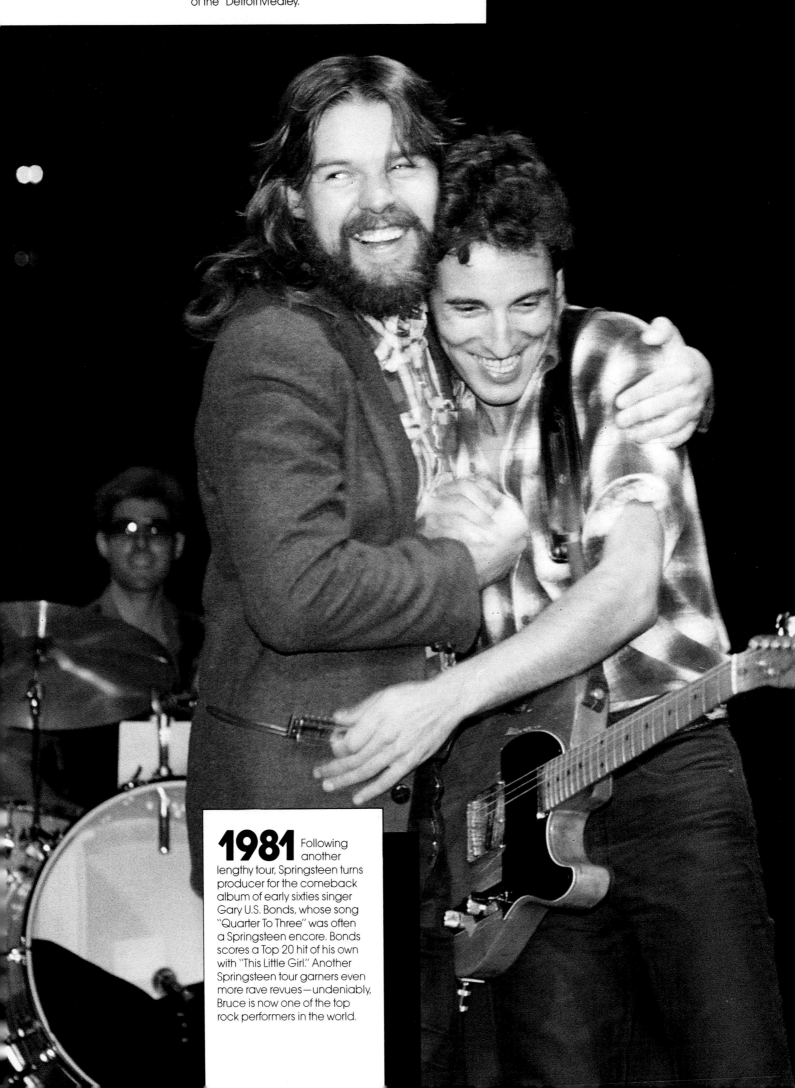

Bob Seger obviously approves of Bruce's performance of the "Detroit Medley."

1981 Following another lengthy tour, Springsteen turns producer for the comeback album of early sixties singer Gary U.S. Bonds, whose song "Quarter To Three" was often a Springsteen encore. Bonds scores a Top 20 hit of his own with "This Little Girl." Another Springsteen tour garners even more rave revues—undeniably, Bruce is now one of the top rock performers in the world.

1982 After a long delay, Springsteen surprises his fans by releasing the all-acoustic album, **Nebraska.** These songs were recorded at his home and were originally intended to serve as demo tapes for the next E Street Band album. Springsteen believes the songs stand on their own merit simply with his vocal performance and guitar accompaniment. Recalling the early folk songs of Bob Dylan and Woody Guthrie, the album does not receive wide-spread air play and the press reaction is mixed because of the stark construction of the songs and melancholy tone of many lyrics. Still, it becomes a Top 5 record.

Bruce's father once gave him this advice: "The guitar is okay as a hobby, but you need something to fall back on. You should be a lawyer."

1983 While working in the studio on his next album, Springsteen also makes sporadic appearances with local bands in the New Jersey Shore area.

"What else do I like besides music? Hmmmm. I'll tell ya . . . not too much besides music. Right now, music is it. I don't care about anything else."

1984 Following an 18-month gap between releases, his seventh album, **Born In The U.S.A.,** is released and reaches #1 within three weeks. The first single "Dancing In The Dark," featuring a modern dance mix by Arthur Baker, goes to #2 in June and becomes Springsteen's biggest-selling single ever. He sets out on an extensive world tour. Miami Steve leaves the E Street Band to work with his own group, Little Steven And The Disciples Of Soul, and is replaced by veteran guitarist Nils Lofgren for the tour. A female background vocalist, Patti Scialfa, is also added. Tickets for Springsteen's ten concerts at New Jersey's Meadowlands Arena—over 200,000 seats in all—sell out in just 24 hours. The second single from **Born In The U.S.A.,** "Cover Me," is released, with the non-LP live track—a Tom Waits song called "Jersey Girl," as the B side. More than a decade after he first reached the public eye, Bruce Springsteen is still undeniably "The Boss."

"The best thing that ever happened to me was when I got thrown out of the first band I was in. I went home and put on 'It's All Over Now' by the Rolling Stones and learned that guitar solo."

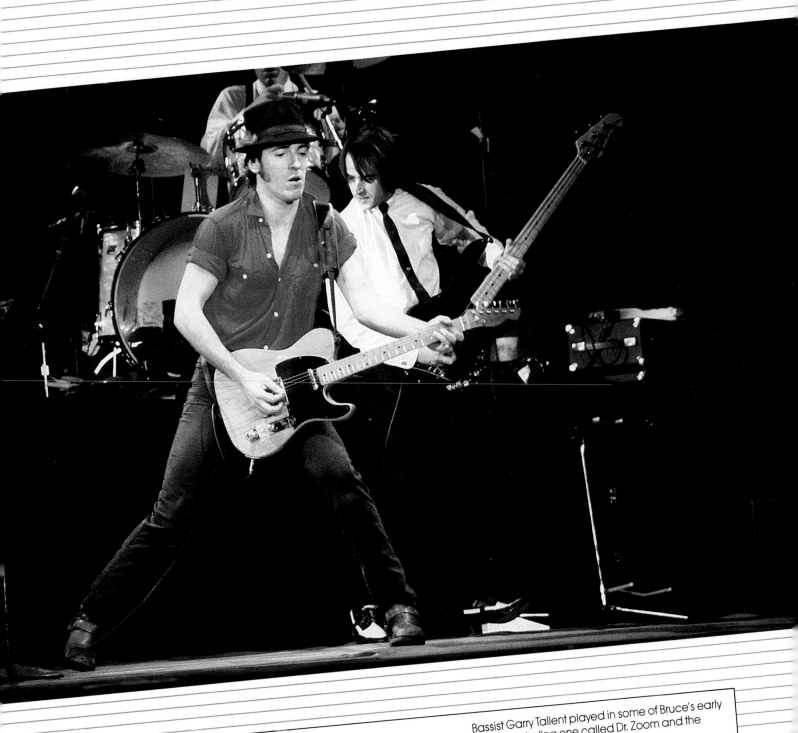

Bassist Garry Tallent played in some of Bruce's early bands, including one called Dr. Zoom and the Sonic Boom.

Bruce began performing the Stones' "Street Fighting Man" during the 1984 tour. Here he demonstrates his street fighting technique.

1984 TOUR

THE BOSS

MICHAEL J. FOX

TIGER BEAT

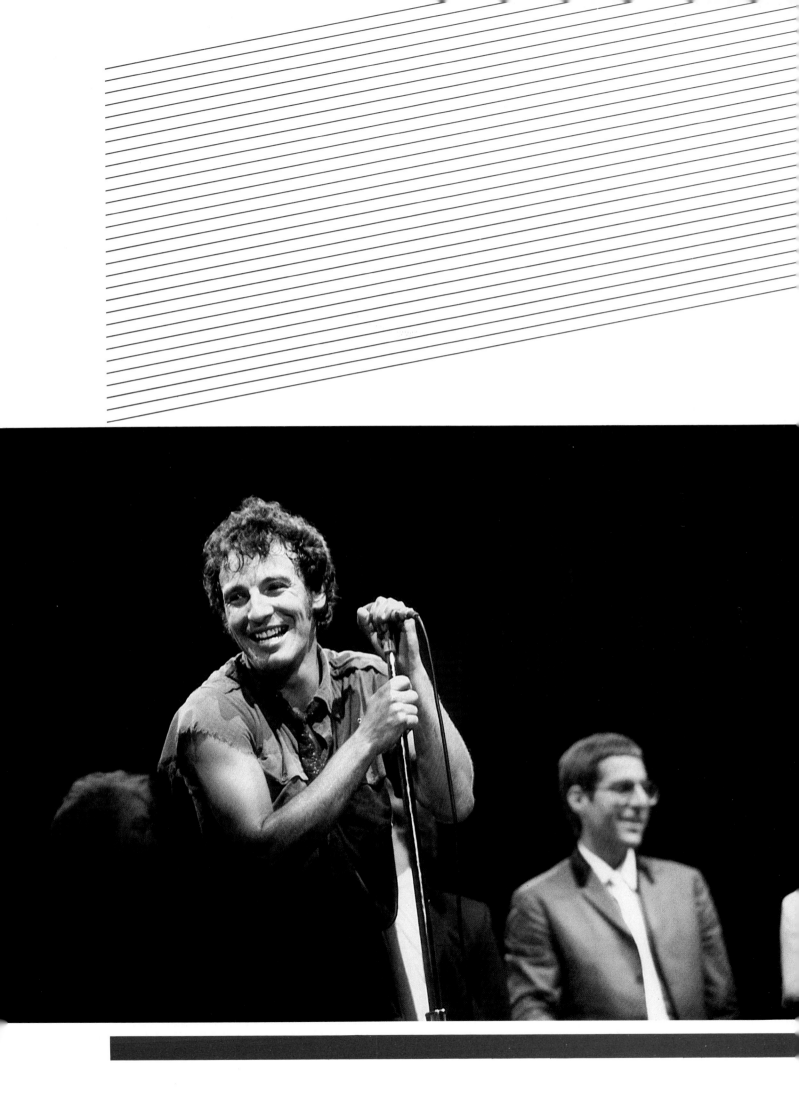

"Rock 'n' roll reaches down into all those homes where there's no music or books or any kind of creative sense, and it infiltrates the whole thing. That's what happened at my house."

MORE FROM THE 1984 TOUR

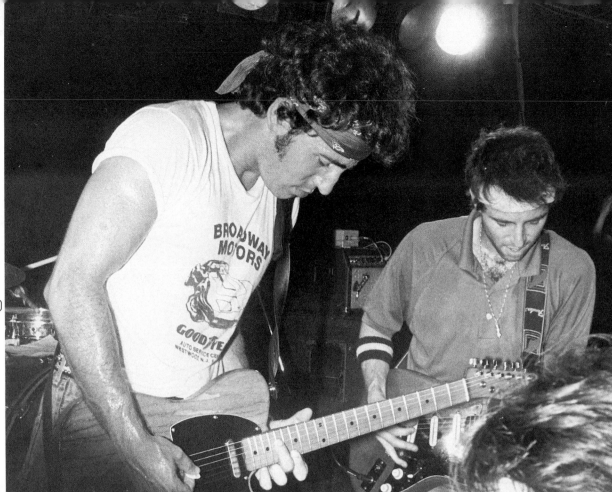

Guitarist Nils Lofgren (right) made his debut with the E Street Band at an unannounced club gig in New Jersey.

He replaced Miami Steve Van Zandt on the 1984 tour.

Tough guys (left to right): The Big Man, The Boss, bassist Garry Tallent, and Miami Steve Van Zandt.

Bruce getting down on an earlier tour.

DISCOGRAPHY

ALBUMS

U.S.	U.K.	Title	Year
Columbia KC 31093	CBS 65480	Greetings From Asbury Park, N.J.	1973
Columbia KC 32432	CBS 65780	The Wild, The Innocent & The E Street Shuffle	1974
Columbia PC 33795	CBS 69170	Born To Run	1975
		(Note: The above album was originally issued in the U.S. with the title written in script lettering. Copies of this record are currently worth nearly $200.)	
Columbia JC 35318	CBS 86061	Darkness On The Edge Of Town	1978
Columbia PC2 36854	CBS 88510	The River	1980
Columbia AS-978 (promo only)	—	Bruce Springsteen As Requested Around The World	1981
Columbia TC 38358	CBS 85669	Nebraska	1982
Columbia PC 38653	CBS 86304	Born In The U.S.A.	1984

Compilation Albums On Which Bruce Springsteen Appears

Columbia A2S-174		The Heavyweights	1975
Elektra/Asylum ML-801		No Nukes	1979
Columbia A2S-890		Hitline '80	1980

SINGLES

U.S.	U.K.	Title	Year
Columbia—Playback 45 (promo only)	—	Blinded By The Light/Avenging Annie (by Andy Pratt)	1972
Columbia 4-45805 (promo only)	—	Blinded By The Light/Blinded By The Light	1973
Columbia 4-45805	—	Blinded By The Light/The Angel	1973
		(Note: The official release of the above record is rarer than the promo. A picture sleeve was also issued and is extremely rare.)	
Columbia 4-45864 (promo only)	—	Spirit In The Night/Spirit In The Night	1973
Columbia 4-45864	—	Spirit In The Night/For You	1973
		(Note: Again, the official release is rarer than the promo of the above record.)	
Columbia 3-10209 (promo only)	—	Born To Run/Born To Run	1975
Columbia 3-10209	CBS 3661	Born To Run/Meeting Across The River	1975
Columbia 3-10274 (promo only)	—	Tenth Avenue Freeze-Out/Tenth Avenue Freeze-Out	1975
Columbia 3-10274	CBS 3840	Tenth Avenue Freeze-Out/She's The One	1975
Columbia 3-10763 (promo only)	—	Prove It All Night/Prove It All Night	1978
Columbia 3-10763	CBS 6424	Prove It All Night/Factory	1978
Columbia 3-10801 (promo only)	—	Badlands/Badlands	1978
Columbia 3-10801	CBS 6532	Badlands/Streets Of Fire	1978
Columbia 11-11391	CBS 9309	Hungry Heart/Held Up Without A Gun	1980
Columbia AS-928 (promo only)	—	Fade Away/Be True/Held Up Without A Gun (12")	1980
—	CBS 9568	Sherry Darling/Be True	1981
Columbia AE7-1332 (promo only)	—	Santa Claus Is Coming To Town/Santa Claus Is Coming To Town	1981
Columbia 11-11431	—	Fade Away/Be True	1981
—	CBS A 1179	The River/Independence Day	1981
—	CBS A 13-1179	The River/Born To Run/Rosalita (12")	1981
—	CBS A 1557	Cadillac Ranch/Wreck On The Highway	1981
—	CBS A 2794	Atlantic City/Mansion On The Hill	1982
—	CBS A 2969	Open All Night/Big Payback	1982
Columbia 38-04463	CBS A 4436	Dancing In The Dark/Pink Cadillac	1984
Columbia 44-05028	—	Dancing In The Dark (Blaster Mix)/Dancing In The Dark (Radio)/Dancing In The Dark (Dub) (12")	1984
Columbia 38-04561	—	Cover Me/Jersey Girl	1984

SPRINGSTEEN PERFORMANCES ON OTHER ARTISTS' RECORDS

GARY U.S. BONDS—Dedication (EMI America, 1981)
  "Jole Blon"—support vocals
  "This Little Girl"—support vocals, guitars and background vocals throughout

CLARENCE CLEMONS AND THE RED BANK ROCKERS—Rescue (Columbia, 1983)
  "Savin' Up"—rhythm guitar

GRAHAM PARKER AND THE RUMOUR—The Up Escalator (Arista, 1980)
  "Endless Night"—support vocals

LOU REED—Street Hassle (Arista, 1978)
  "Street Hassle"—narration

DONNA SUMMER—Donna Summer (Geffen, 1982)
  "Protection"—guitar, featured solo

HOW TO CONTACT BRUCE SPRINGSTEEN
c/o Columbia Records
51 W. 52nd St.
New York, N.Y. 10019

There are two fanzines written by and for the hardcore Bruce fan, which are worth looking into.

THUNDER ROAD
P.O. Box 171
Bogota, N.J. 07603

Although Thunder Road is no longer published, back issues of this glossy, informative publication are still available and highly recommended for those seeking additional information on Bruce, the E Street Band, Southside Johnny, and the Asbury Park scene.

BACKSTREETS
P.O. Box 51225
Seattle, WA 98115

Quarterly tabloid with interesting regular features, international discographies, news updates, and collectors' classifieds.

There are also three fanzines published in England, available by subscription.
These are:

CANDY'S ROOM
c/o Gary Desmond
74, Winskill Road
Liverpool L11 1HB
England

POINT BLANK
c/o Dan French
11a, Thirlmere Road
London SW 16
England

THE FEVER
c/o Percival
66 Norman Place Rd.
Keresley
Coventry
CV6 2BT
England